# Paradise on Earth with Words

# Paradise on Earth with Words

## Collection 2: Social Society

Eric Scott Grand

Eric Scott Grand has been writing poetry for the last thirty years. He has attended poetry symposiums and recorded songs. His work has been previously published in anthologies. Grand lives and writes by the majestic Pacific Ocean in Carlsbad, California. This is his second collection.

All rights reserved. No part of this publication may be reproduced, distributed, or transmitted in any form by any means, including photocopying, recording, or other electronic methods without the prior written permission of the author, except in the case of brief quotations embodied in reviews and certain other noncommercial uses permitted by copyright law. For permission requests, write to the author at the address below.

Copyright © 2022 Eric Scott Grand

ericscottgrand@gmail.com
www.ericscottgrand.wixsite.com/website

ISBN 978-0-578-94636-8

Edited and designed by Tell Tell Poetry

Printed in the United States of America

First Printing, 2022

To my parents for giving me the opportunity
to have the experiences I've had
and to go the places I've been,
which made this collection possible.

# Contents

## Making Friends & Having Fun — 1
Social Butterfly — 3
Socialize — 4
Social Scene — 5
Sociable — 6
Social Venue — 7
Social Function — 8
A Social Affair — 9

## Staying Connected — 11
All Too Social — 13
Social Media — 14
Social Buzz — 15
Social Views — 16
Social Trends — 17

## Climbing the Social Ladder — 19
Social Level — 21
Social Relations — 22
A Social Network — 23
Social Standards — 24
High Society — 26
Socialites — 27
Social Values — 28

## Taking Care of Ourselves — 29
Social Ties — 31
Social Matters — 32
Antisocial — 33
Social Distancing — 34
Social Binds — 35

## Taking Care of Each Other — 37
Social Situations — 39

| | |
|---|---|
| Social Diversity | 40 |
| Social Needs | 41 |
| Social Justice | 42 |

# Making Friends
& Having Fun

# Social Butterfly

Part of what it does is harmless fun
It has a friendly personality it can talk
About any subject that comes up without
Hesitation that it shows in verbal communication
That it can handle any situation that it comes by
It's a social butterfly who knows how to break
The ice when it's too quiet that has a broad
Vocabulary that hardly ever stumbles over words
That doesn't mumble to explain what it describes
It's a social butterfly that speaks clearly takes its
Time to do it repeatedly patiently to be friendly
With a kind gesture that can find ways to comply
It's a social butterfly

Has a gift for gab that's good to ask for advice
It's a social butterfly that sounds energized less
Tired in other instances it communicates freely
Constantly that has a purpose to talk if it's just
To greet it can turn out more than brief that's
Not shy it's a social butterfly that has a talent
To blab has an eager character that knows how
To approach be presentable when in a normal
Formal environment it's a social butterfly

It's easier for it to adapt be street-savvy when
Outdoors it learns more is helpful knowledgeable
When outside it's a social butterfly that knows
How to get along with anyone who is not scared
To express itself in a crowd with diverse words
Is not afraid to say what's on its mind it's a social
Butterfly when it gets to a point it has a way to
Explain what it means to make more sense to say
It right it's a social butterfly

# Socialize

It's made for conversation to analyze
We socialize when there's time to spare
Nothing to interfere with no one to interrupt
That deals with several topics that come up
All at once to compromise we socialize
One-on-one that covers different subjects
At the same time that's rational done casual
That comes natural if you're practical to get
Along with everyone to realize we socialize

It's used for communication to share
What takes place with dialogue we socialize
To listen give your opinion your perspective
That's of interest with analytical feedback
That's exact that can be words that are wise
We socialize it's done to handle situations
So there won't be complications later to
Reassure there won't be disputes to have
No need to apologize we socialize that's
Done to pass the time to inform to not
Be bored to be heard to find out what's
Known have a common ground not criticize
We socialize

It's done to exchange information that's
Time set aside to prioritize we socialize
To have a sit-down to ask to tell to say
This and that have a chitchat to laugh be
Nice we socialize to say what's on your
Mind in your free time to act normal seems
Casual to be happy that is right we socialize

# Social Scene

It shows your true self your wealth health
When you're able to go out among bystanders
Share their emotional feelings when you're seen
In the social scene sometimes you watch over time
To get someone's attention if not be discreet
By looking in another direction someone needs
To make a move to further continue

When in a group there's something to prove
When you're alone it shows you're in control
If you don't act fast there won't be a second chance
People are more cooperative when you're talkative
That is friendly in the social scene words are exchanged
Thoughts are explained voices are heard all at once it's
Easier to get along to have a talk one-on-one to feel at
Ease in the social scene

It demonstrates your personality mentality
Preferably when it's evening in the social scene
To have a conversation find something in
Common with someone to relate that you're
Able to meet in the social scene it can go
Smoothly if agreed easily where a spot can
Be found to have a sit-down to speak in the
Social scene

It makes known what you're about your interests
Likes dislikes your type is right how you're perceived
It's the social scene where there's more than meets
The eye if there are good vibes it's not hard to approach
Who you're interested in the most without fear in the social
Scene it makes curious less worrisome what takes place
For entertainment place wagers personal favors that's
Exciting to be in the social scene

# Sociable

It shows you're apt to adapt that makes
It comfortable that's normal when you're sociable
In an awkward situation it's good to have communication
For business relations to keep a client distracted before a
Meeting starts that's an opportunity that won't be a loss
That's negotiable when you're sociable there's more to
Say feel like when there's time to wait before an appointment
It makes it easy to speak freely without interruption discussion
Not put on guilt that makes it difficult to express what they
Mean to say not be hesitant in any way that prevents what's
Meant to be said that's not impossible when you're sociable

When there's dialogue it's a conversation
To share information to get along keep calm
Be heard speaking words when you're sociable
It makes minutes go by fast when you're able to talk
Thoughts viewpoints that sound familiar
That may be similar to share what's in common
To overcome problems that you're supposed to
When you're sociable you're recognized identified
Acknowledged often you're given attention
Your name is mentioned you're listened to with interest
You're given time to say what's on your mind
To share an opinion on what was said then better explain
What was meant from experiences you've had
That's local when you're sociable

It demonstrates you're able to communicate
To adjust that's moral when you're sociable
You'll go to new places see different faces
With the right attitude it's easy to show gratitude
Open with compliments when you're out and about
When you stay mobile when you're sociable
In a function environment it's a requirement
To get by survive get accustomed to know someone
Versatile when you're sociable

# Social Venue

It's outdoors where people go
It's a social venue it makes ways
To pass the time with like minds
That share interests the place they visit
For instance a performance show
It's a social venue that can be meant
To enjoy mostly with entertainment
Where there could be a festival celebration
With places that offer food that patrons
Can order from a menu it's a social venue

It happens in public where many can attend
That gives them something to do
It's a social venue it would be preferable
To see people in their prime to go somewhere
Where they feel alive to get the attention
To be mentioned to feel special it's a social venue
Where it's possible to participate to be
On a video monitor to relive a moment
For amusement to view it's a social venue

It takes place in a selected area
That several can attend that's free
Also reserved it's a social venue
They have places to lounge while
Sitting down alone it could also
Be in groups it's a social venue
That's allowed permission to go
With a fee admission that has restrictions
With rules regulations that the experience
Can be new it's a social venue

# Social Function

It's planned out on a specific date it takes place
That can be important it's a social function
Where it's expected to get dressed up
To be presentable that's respectable
By invitation you're able to gain entrance
To attend a benefit to build relations with strangers
That's an option it's a social function
That's on schedule it can be a moment
That's special it's a social function

It's done by reservation to commemorate
It can go on till it gets late with no disruptions
It's a social function that advertises
Is full of surprises to expect who could be
In attendance friends colleagues associates
To reminisce also talk about what's current
It's a social function it takes place
In public locations to give donations
For payments where people have introductions
It's a social function

It's a special occasion to show appreciation
Where guests can relax with alcohol consumption
It's a social function that allows them to find a place
To have their space where being glamorous
Is practiced it's a social function
Where you're able to look your very best
To impress to be a topic for discussion
It's a social function

# A Social Affair

We noticed each other after which I approached
It was not a formal introduction just casual conversation
Between acquaintances in the free time we had to spare
In a social affair we later became friends
To speak about our interests how we feel
That appeals to us that's fun we find each other funny
That we enjoy each other's company we take long walks
To talk that we speak about our experiences
That we have concerns that we express how we care
In a social affair we communicate our problems
That we have in common we try to get to know each other
When we're together we help one another
Whenever possible to not get in trouble
In order to treat each one of us fair in a social affair

We watched one another later out of curiosity
I spoke took a hands-on approach to make my point
When I had thoughts to share in a social affair
I try to say whatever I can come up with that's kind
Any time I remembered something to mention
I wouldn't hesitate to acknowledge it in a second
If I had a compliment to give I would let it be known
Quick sometimes I wonder from a distance
What goes on through your mind what it ponders
When I see that your eyes stare in a social affair
I attempt to do my best to make an impression
To be remembered so you're aware in a social affair

We looked in each other's direction then I went closer
To where you were in a seat I sat I asked random questions
That were of some interest that we could relate
It was in a hurry that brought up a bit of a worry on your part
That I wanted to say to begin with so you're prepared
In a social affair over time I came up with something
To talk about to see if we had anything in common

To find a relation we could compare in a social affair
The moments we spent have allowed for us to be friends
That's an advantage we can manage like a couple pair
In a social affair

ered Connected
# Staying Connected

# All Too Social

It can be used at your own pace
With no use of vocal cords it's all too social
It's easy to explain with letters in case
It's mispronounced if not heard it makes it
Convenient to text messages for long distance
Communication that makes it easier than speaking
Out loud when there may be disruptive sounds
In the background that can be done when mobile
It's all too social it's a handheld device to hold
Close it's all too social

It's a technological wonder that runs at a high rate
That's less cost to wait for a long response
Than it does on a landline that has a dial tone
It's all too social it has applications for entertainment
To stay busy on your own it's all too social it has a network
To purchase products for payment that's portable
It's all too social

It's lightweight for carrying it can be utilized
To organize lives it comes equipped with programs
Built into it to keep the mind occupied when alone
It's all too social it can be good company
Whenever no one is there to accompany
When bored it's all too social
That gives an advantage when stranded
There's no need to panic when your location
Can be found exact if the area you're in is local
It's all too social

# Social Media

Communication that travels long distances
For people to read on social media
Where you're able to leave comments confess problems
Share concerns get helpful advice in return
Post words to reply then say what's on your mind
To see on social media they're messages
That can be responded to from far away
That can be delivered in a matter of seconds
For it to be viewed repeatedly on social media

Information that moves instantaneously
For people to look closely on social media
Where you're able to give your opinion
It's a click away for it to be displayed
Right away pressed with the tip of your finger
That can be done quickly on social media
That's useful for reference to be aware
That can help for later use there are ways
To play games that involve trivia on social media

Mass amounts of data that operate at a high speed
For recreational means can be experienced
On social media there are ways to search
For research what's enjoyed to learn more
About your interests what makes you curious
To study on social media where there's more
To explore when needing to know see on social media

# Social Buzz

Part of it is what happens currently
That's spoken of it's a social buzz
That stays it won't go away until a new topic
Comes up that's repeated enough it's a social buzz
That develops to communicate speculate
Until further is heard to put into words
Together with facts what took place in the past
To discover what's right wrong it's a social buzz

It includes what goes on presently how it's told
It's a social buzz it spreads quickly how it's
Mentioned catches people's attention
It continues to make people talk it's a social buzz
It happens by chance accident it could be passed on
By others who know how it's explained
Can decide what course it will take
It's hard to expect which will be said more
When it's too much it's a social buzz

It involves what occurs lately that's daily
That's discussed it's a social buzz it's the latest news
That's out it becomes public after it's uncovered
How long it remains depends on how much
It could not be forgotten it's a social buzz
It turns into a subject to clear matters up in person
If it's withheld there are other ways for it to be
Known it can go global it's a social buzz

# Social Views

They're based on opinions that are partly true
They're social views they have different sides
To decide what's right in your mind
You're able to dispute however there's a point
It can confuse if you're not sure what to do
They're social views that give advice to convince
On the condition you're able to choose
They're social views

They look at all possibilities after they're gathered
What you're able to determine to conclude
They're social views that have to be researched
To know the specifics to get the answers sought
To be truth they're social views that give an option
To function later at your own pace
When you've got to its root they're social views

They take into consideration all information
Questioned till you realize what is new
They're social views looking into makes it known
Then can be found out on your own that you're able
To pursue they're social views according to belief
You'll have to see to believe then come to
Your own conclusion what's suitable
They're social views

# Social Trends

They have an outlook to see what's ahead
They're social trends there are percentages rates
That escalate fluctuate that are of interest
For futurists realists for finances it could be
How much to spend they're social trends
It's a point of view what's gonna be new
Further down the road that has not yet been old
That can be a wave of the future that's talked about
With family friends they're social trends

They give an idea of what's to come
Based on financial expenses they're social trends
They have ratio statistics that can be both optimistic
And pessimistic that's a field of study for economists
Forecasters so minor setbacks could be prevented
They're social trends it's market research that determines
What to look for change that's part of what is meant
They're social trends

It shows what to expect further later than lately happens
They're social trends that are of interest to decide
What's right in the marketplace to buy
What's a popular item for purchase that's spent
They're social trends they give a perspective
Of logistics by modernists to make forward progress
That's best they're social trends

# Climbing the Social Ladder

# Social Level

It's measured on an even scale that's debatable
Reliable dependable lived on a social level
With the people to meet the company to keep
That's maintained not to lose sight of what side to take
In order to treat equally accounts for the hours
To stay awake how long you'll be up late

If there's no hurry you'll be home early
If there's a deadline you'll be up late to not fail
Keeping it on a social level that gets unbalanced
If not prioritized right if you're not organized
It will go in a downward spiral for a while
Until it decides to be stable will keep it
On a social level

It's how time is used effectively in a manner
That's correct to get your affairs in order
To do what you're capable of on a social level
To do what has to be done with the quantity
Amount that you're able on a social level
It's getting enough done evenly to be kept
On schedule to be on a social level

It's calculated to be fair
Managing how matters are handled
That every encounter has to be treated
With the utmost respect that's special
When it's on a social level if it's done
How it's meant it won't put you over the edge

If it's excessive it could wind up a big expense
If not made aware to share if it doesn't turn out fair
It could tip over as if it were on a scale
When it applies to a social level it's estimated
It can levitate as much as if put on a pedestal
When it's on a social level

# Social Relations

It's hard to make a career to live out your dreams
Sometimes it just falls into place if there's
Communication with social relations
It starts at an early age where you've been
Who you've seen that reflects the image to project
To gain respect to try to avoid certain situations
With social relations you're best off to finish
What you've started keep problems to a minimum
Go about your business share your interests
Where it won't be repeated that it's enough said
Mentioned with social relations

It's difficult to survive to get by
Sometimes you'll have to take risks to exist
Show what you're capable of prove what you're able
To do use your imagination with social relations
It's better not to show too much concern about
What you're not to know trust can be lost
If spoken too much when not involved in the conversation
With social relations when caught in the middle
Of a discussion that you're not part of
It's better to retreat leave without indication
With social relations

It's a challenge to come through what you're meant to do
With the right motivation appointed to an exact location
You can be headed towards the right direction with social relations
Taking others' advice builds character to encourage later
To have confidence that shows some consideration
With social relations it's best not to overreact about
What has developed in the past that contradicts
Leads to conflict being quiet to stay silent
Makes it less violent for your protection
With social relations

# A Social Network

Every person has a part to do for no one to lose
Who has an area of expertise to achieve
What they need to receive there won't be a loss
If the timing is not off for a reward
By a social network everyone can reach success
If they do their best to apply what they know
To reach their goal by a social network
It's a team effort to turn out better
Without one's specialty the others
Can't function effectively to deserve
What they earn by a social network

Every person has to participate in some way
In order to get paid the most by a social network
Each one has a special skill that they specialize in
To capitalize the time they invest to turn out correct
By a social network individuals who are organized
To keep their eyes on a prize who come up with a plan
To get what they intend with each other's help
By a social network

Every person has to be a participant
To come out a winner with the talents
They acquired to end up with what they desire
If they hit their mark they can get what they want
Something in return by a social network
It's a group involvement to get results that count
That can amount to wealth no one will lose
If everyone comes to an agreement they approve
That won't hurt them at all by a social network
If everyone cooperates there will be no mistakes
If everyone abides it will turn out alright
Without trouble by a social network

# Social Standards

It's rated by the way you live once you're established
They're social standards how you're raised determines
Later how to behave the influences you're adapted to
Categorize what affluence you're accustomed to
If you have good etiquette later you can benefit from it
What you thought first will show what you've known
Before you're grown how you're able to treat others
Can be repaid in numbers on how good your manners are
They're social standards the conditions you live in
Will determine how much later to return to give
If it's abundant it's more than enough
They're social standards

It's a status grade recognized by the public
They're social standards the condition you're in
Decides later how sure you are about decisions
Depending on your upbringing will return back
Memories the environment you're in determines
How positive your confidence will be
Effective in your pursuits that you're meant to do
How you're able to approach a problem from a distance
Will help improve later how to reach that objective
The people you come in contact with can predict
How you'll behave act at times to find ways to adapt
They're social standards the company kept will determine
What's in your best interest if there's a threat
They're there to protect your relationships
That can harm they're social standards

It's a category based on finance that you're placed in
By class they're social standards after you've found
What you're able to easily grasp what follows
Comes natural matters seem simple when you're able
To pinpoint what you're good at that you're able to develop
They're social standards after there's no need for assistance

You're proficient once you're able to discover the limits
Of your conditions then you're able to decide
How it's mastered they're social standards

# High Society

To advance fast to not end up last
For responsibility in high society
To reach a status level that's incredible
With privilege benefits added incentives
That makes it exclusive that you're able
To be lucrative in your pursuits
To have good attributes for opportunities
In high society to get ahead do your best
To help humanity in high society

To rise above come out on top financially
In high society to gain escalate with a situation
That's a fortune in your endeavors
With well-deserved bonuses included
For services in philanthropy in high society
To be the first to have wealth a net worth
To generate revenue that's substantial in value
A lump sum of money in high society

To compete defeat for popularity in high society
To amount to a large income that counts
With perks earned through work in excursions
For your diversion for stability in high society
To have success in excess that you're able to profit
Off your investments for infinite possibilities
In high society

# Socialites

They're social people that's what they specialize in
They're socialites where they attend receptions
To know someone new who is introduced there
In attendance are persons of importance
Such as dignitaries luminaries royalty among them
Are guests they're socialites accustomed
To talk about a topic of what they do with the public
To be lucrative to live the way they like they're socialites

They go to events where people mingle
Spend time to wine dine they're socialites
Who attend conventions fundraising benefits
With people of means to be seen
They keep up with trends to share interests
They learn customs for formal introductions
They stay in touch with the times for others
To give opinions to say what's on their mind
They're socialites they have a fashion sense
To compliment how people dress they live a lifestyle
That's worthwhile with surprises of excitement
With the people they come across who live
Interesting lives they're socialites

They go out at night they're socialites
Who go to extravagant gala premieres
Who wear the finest luxuries who go to parties
That can take place late they're socialites
Who greet and meet who's there by invitation
Individuals with status reputation such as celebrities
Emissaries excellencies who are nearby
When they arrive they're socialites

# Social Values

They're taught after birth while in the process
Of growing up they're social values they're repeated
By your family told by those who care the most
Like your parents after several times said it becomes a habit
While you're being raised developing what makes sense
With ethics then situations are easier to handle
They're social values their positive effects build respect
That seems to be natural they're social values

They're told repeatedly when forgotten easily over time
They seem to get old not new they're social values
They become routine after it's seen how to be done correctly
They reflect on how well you focus your manners
What you're accustomed to they're social values
They show in instances when you're not to be involved
In a conversation if it's no concern of yours
You're better off not to intrude they're social values

They're learned with examples they're social values
They demonstrate how well you're educated in your etiquette
That will let you get approval they're social values
They will help build relations with less hesitation
If applied to decide it can determine your attitude
What actions can be learned through what others do
They're social values

# Taking Care of Ourselves

# Social Ties

It takes up your time when there's much on the mind
But company makes it alright with social ties
There's support in case you're emotionally hurt
To calm if you're alarmed to do no harm
Have less tension to regroup reevaluate to see why
With social ties there are more ways than one
To overcome problems that are hard to identify
With social ties

It's where you're able to go when emotions
Are bottled up inside with social ties you're able
To get more insight with the people by your side
They can help guide to help you feel fine
With social ties there's less to worry about not much
To be in a hurry about when on edge they can relieve
Stress aggravation that makes you impatient
To lower your tone before matters get out of control
Then emotions are set aside with social ties

It can prevent overreactions it can alleviate
A bad temperament that's what it signifies with
Social ties are those who you're able to rely on most
Who are trustworthy who keep in touch closely
When lonely when worried look for added security
At some times with social ties there's no concern
Where to turn to go for moral support
When it's nearby with social ties

# Social Matters

They're open for discussions to overcome problems
They're social matters when an issue needs to be dealt
A solution to find help one who can diagnose
Who knows an antidote someone in a profession
Who can deal with situations such as frustration
Depression isolation for treatment to be obedient
Practical they're social matters to speak freely about
Concerns that cause emotional hurt that pose
Trouble it's better to seek a person who specializes
To be less traumatized who can handle they're
Social matters

To consult with a specialist who's a therapist
To analyze for a therapy that's practiced
They're social matters professionally
That's medically proven for health conditions
With assistance who can be a counselor practitioner
They're social matters who offer their services
If you've developed a bad habit they're
Social matters

To deal with issues that are personal
They're social matters it's normally one-on-one
By appointment for a private moment that may require
Getting a prescription for medication to prevent injury
An accident they're social matters to find a discovery
For a slow recovery that's hard to endure
To find a cure that's logical they're
Social matters

# Antisocial

They keep to themselves who are less verbal
They're antisocial they maintain their distance
They show no interest don't talk much
Don't do enough don't like to participate in events
They'd rather stay home they're antisocial
They find it best to be in a quiet place that's private
To be isolated to escape hate be safe from what aggravates
What builds more stress than there already is
It encourages them to find other ways to deal with it
That's personal they're antisocial

An individual who spends time alone
Who has no care what goes on in the world
They're antisocial who would rather be indoors not being mobile
Who doesn't confide who prefers to know
What counts on the inside who makes a choice
Of their own they're antisocial if they have a prerogative
They have a reason not to be talkative not to be unkind
They may have a lot on their mind to help them stay
Focused for a purpose that's important who don't want
To draw unnecessary attention to themselves
They're antisocial

Someone who's not accustomed to attachment
Normally trying to avoid conflict situations
They go where they can keep their concentration
Where it seems normal they're antisocial
They don't like where there's energy that's negative
Where they feel uncomfortable they're antisocial
It turns out better for them not to be disturbed so no one
Will be offended if for a reason there are misinterpreted
Words they're antisocial

# Social Distancing

It keeps us isolated with not many to communicate
With who can be hard to reach it's social distancing
You're not able to stand close it's recommended to
Stay indoors preferably you're home you're not able
To be near to speak it's social distancing it's suggested
To be six feet apart not have physical contact in public
Outdoors it's to prevent getting infected it's better to
Wear a mask wash your hands sanitize to be on the
Safe side to stay clean it's social distancing

It draws a line to stand in a spot if caught someone
Will point to a mark it doesn't let you get too close
Next to the opposite sex it can get annoying it's
Social distancing emotional feelings could be
Misinterpreted if not aware at the moment the
Purpose for actions by someone who feels they
Have an attraction they're missing it's social
Distancing it rains on your parade for your
Plans for the day if it involves going where
You're able to do more than being alone
Resting it's social distancing

It makes us stay separate too much space for affection
Reasons it's social distancing it doesn't permit us to hold hands
With loved ones if seen it might be first warned then
Enforced for safety it helps to have the proper gear
To eliminate fear it's social distancing it sets boundaries
That are mandatory in order not to contract a virus
That spreads like wildfire until everyone has got the
Vaccine it's social distancing

# Social Binds

It's when you're close with someone
Who shows their concern the most who
Likes to know what's on your mind they're
Social binds they come to your aid when
You're in pain who have the patience to let
You describe it they're social binds all they
Want is to help when you don't seem well
They mean the best to make it less negative
To make it turn out fine they're social binds

It's a vow made between people to treat each
Other fairly when they grow up through hard
Times they're social binds they show devotion
To the ones they worry about the most don't
Desert abandon who can be a daughter son
Relative family friend those you can depend
On that's right they're social binds who calm
Your nerves when you're hurt even when they
Seem busy they put all aside they're social binds

It's a strong bond with someone formed when young
Who worries when you're not alright they're social
Binds who put all their energy toward your safety
Your well-being to not fall behind they're social
Binds who are supportive and protective that give
Encouragement to guide they're social binds

# Taking Care of Each Other

# Social Situations

When there's a problem that needs to be discussed
It's best to confront it be up-front not withhold
Information in social situations what serves
Right to decide how to deal with it do it at the
Moment it's spoken it's important how it's phrased
Mentioned in social situations it's best to absorb
What's heard before giving a response in spoken
Words exchanging back and forth to get a viewpoint
That has no misinterpretation in social situations

When there's an issue that needs to be addressed
It's better to be direct not be hesitant if you keep it
Bottled up inside it can reflect on the outside
It changes your behavior which can lead to confrontations
In social situations it's better to prepare what you're
Gonna say to listen prior to giving your version of events
To prevent any more mistakes that may take place if words
Are out of context that disrespect without hesitation in social
Situations you're better off when your thoughts are kept to
Yourself when not part of a conversation in social situations

When there's a matter to clear up it would be
In your interest to deal with it knowing how
Best to approach won't let it get out of control
What is said can make a difference between right
And wrong to decide if you're emotionally strong
With determination in social situations it puts to the
Challenge what you're able to manage to solve a
Problem to find a solution that's your obligation
In social situations it involves courage to not be discouraged
To end up with enjoyment does not have disappointment
With misleading directions in social situations

# Social Diversity

When they all gather in one place to get emotional
Like in a rally it's social diversity they have
The same feelings for healing in different ethnicities
It's social diversity that includes people in groups
Who share what they know to improve be good
Show their support not have adversity it's social
Diversity they come together with the intention
To make things better for peace prosperity it's
Social diversity

It includes people of different beliefs that
Have the same meaning based on race creed
It's social diversity that varies in standards
Demographic types that have similarities with
Slight differences from a majority it's social
Diversity that has to do with individuals who
All have a like interest in mind that has different
Ways to be explained independently it's
Social diversity

It deals with individuals who want the same result
It first draws confusion then ends up in a peaceful
Solution that began with controversy it's social
Diversity that leaves in bewilderment after it finishes
In agreement on equal standards that seem unlikely
It's social diversity when many get together for an
Event for example that will take place there's uncertainty
What will happen it's social diversity

# Social Needs

They're necessities to properly succeed
They're social needs automobiles vehicles jobs
For transportation costs forms of identity to be
Presented legally numerical codes to pursue a
Career are social needs that require you to have
A bank account credit cards not to make it hard
To pay any other way immediately they're social
Needs to make a living keep on giving for medical
Expenses for conditions to prevent disease
They're social needs

They're requirements to move forward proceed
They're social needs items for communication
An education shelter to reside to be inside a place
To feel safe for security they're social needs
An identity to be identified cash that's plenty
Healthcare insurance for faster service to be healthy
They're social needs

They're essential in one way to lead they're social needs
Ways to move around to keep your feet off the ground
With identification to travel with a passport
To be secured financially to purchase appliances
That run on electricity they're social needs
To have academic credentials to be flexible
For immediate employment to have stability
They're social needs

# Social Justice

It gives people the freedom to speak out
The best they can express in a protest for
Equality after a tragedy that expects a more
Positive outcome it's social justice it's to take
A stand in times that are bad it's needed to change
Ways to be better than before that must not go on it's
Social justice that allows the public to exercise their
Rights in moments of difficulty not be kept separately
It's responsible to show who's accountable
Not just continue to be tragic it's social justice

It gives permission for the public to do their civic duty
For unity to participate without punishment
It's social justice where there's a rally for citizens
With similar interests to stop what they don't want
That's proper procedure to make us aware of community leaders
Who are callous who do acts out of malice that later
It's believed they're not to be trusted it's social justice
That permits us to have a public demonstration to complain
What shouldn't have taken place under the authorities' watch
It's social justice

It authorizes us to take action against what was wrong
It's social justice it's a human right that's an alternative solution
To fighting if it's nonviolently it can end quietly when done it's
Social justice it's a movement for improvement to resolve what's
Outlawed to have problems be gone it's social justice

www.ingramcontent.com/pod-product-compliance
Lightning Source LLC
Chambersburg PA
CBHW032018290426
44109CB00013B/713